KEY SURVIVAL THROUGH TRADING CHAOS

IN 5 EXERCISES, BECOME A PROFITABLE TRADER WITH SIMPLIFIED STRATEGIES

START YOUR TRADING JOURNEY!

IRVIN ELLISON

Text Copyright © IRVIN ELLISON

All rights reserved. No part of this guide may be reproduced in any form without permission in writing from the publisher except in the case of brief quotations embodied in critical articles or reviews.

Legal & Disclaimer

The information contained in this book and its contents is not designed to replace or take the place of any form of medical or professional advice; and is not meant to replace the need for independent medical, financial, legal or other professional advice or services, as may be required. The content and information in this book has been provided for educational and entertainment purposes only.

The content and information contained in this book has been compiled from sources deemed reliable, and it is accurate to the best of the Author's knowledge, information and belief. However, the Author cannot guarantee its accuracy and validity and cannot be held liable for any errors and/or omissions. Further, changes are periodically made to this book as and when needed. Where appropriate and/or necessary, you must consult a professional (including but not limited to your doctor, attorney, financial advisor or such other professional advisor) before using any of the suggested remedies, techniques, or information in this book.

Upon using the contents and information contained in this book, you agree to hold harmless the Author from and against any damages, costs, and expenses, including any legal fees potentially resulting from the application of any of the information provided by this book. This disclaimer applies to any loss, damages or injury caused by the use and application, whether directly or indirectly, of any advice or information presented, whether for breach of contract, tort, negligence, personal injury, criminal intent, or under any other cause of action.

You agree to accept all risks of using the information presented inside this book.

You agree that by continuing to read this book, where appropriate and/or necessary, you shall consult a professional (including but not limited to your doctor, attorney, or financial advisor or such other advisor as needed) before using any of the suggested remedies, techniques, or information in this book.

Table of Contents

Introduction   1

Chapter 1   3

The Top Priority Decision You Need To Make For Your Profitability   3

    Social Opinion Analysis   3
    Rollercoaster Trading and Risk Tolerance Approach   4
    Trading System of Law   4
    Oscillating Trading   5
    Maximizing Your Money Per Trade   8
    Activity #1   10
    Answers for Activity #1   11

Chapter 2   13

The #1 Mistake You May Make Which Kills Your Profits   13

    The Strategy of Scheduling Options   14
    Price Action and Profitability   14
    Trading Edge Over the Market   15
    Low-Risk Options Trading Strategy   16
    High-Profit Probability Options Trading Strategy   17
    Be a Fortune Teller by Using Price and Volume   18
    Activity #2   20

Answer for Activity #2 21

Chapter 3 22

Ultimate Bargain Hunter 22

Trading Crude Oil and Natural Gas 22
Trading With Time-Bard 23
Stock and Forex Trading 25
Activity #3 26
Answers for Activity #3 27

Chapter 4 28

Money That Loses Trades 28

The #1 Mistake Approach 28
The #1 Negligence You May Have Made 29
Slow Down Your Pace 30
Swing Trading 31
The Technique to Avoid Pitfalls 32
Activity #4 33
Answers for Activity #4 34

Chapter 5 35

Strategy of Payment 35

Reading Order Flow 35
Unusual Option Activity 37
    The OCRRBTT Trading Plan 37

Perks of Scheduled Options	38
Maximize Your Profits in the Earning Season	39
Four-Step Earning Season Profit Plan	39
Trading Edge in Simple Steps	40
Activity #5	42
Answers for Activity #5	43
Conclusion	**44**
Review Time	**45**

Introduction

Almost all people are interested in figuring out how to grow their wealth. One of the ways you can do this is by being a profitable trader! Standard terms like *"Plan your Trade right; Trade your Plan"* or *"Make sure to Maintain your Profit"* might appear as a distraction instead of dependable information. Hence, those new traders only desire to figure out how to set-up their charts with the primary purpose of generating some money quickly.

If you are a new trader wanting to get started in trading without good information, it will be tough! Want to save your time and achieve profits without difficulty? You need to understand which simplified trading techniques work in the real markets.

So, let me help you find out which strategies best suit you!

The biggest question is: Can anyone become a successful trader?

YES!

There is only one small caution for this: You have to have the **motivation** to be successful.

Common mistakes which many traders make is that they neglect their strategy and trying to outmaneuver the markets. They refuse to give up on pre-existing ideas and also overlook the "traditional knowledge". New traders tend to intersect the rationality of what the market must do with the truth of how the market is performing. Well, the good news is that these kinds of issues can be fixed by understanding how the markets actually work and accepting them.

The essential move to being a successful trader is that you need to understand which trading strategies best suit you. Every single trader might have different types of trading strategies that are able to meet all their needs and requirements. Make sure that you choose the most suitable trading strategy to stand out as a successful trader.

Chapter 1

The Top Priority Decision You Need To Make For Your Profitability

Using a company's perspective as an example, the concern of leaders in a company is achieving goals and making high profits. The management makes decisions by considering the perspective and needs of the customer. These decisions are based on the condition and personality of the company developers. So, as an individual, you need to find compatible trading strategies that suit you as each individual has different personalities and needs.

So, here are some trading strategies that you need to understand.

Social Opinion Analysis

Traders' views and ideas can be articulated online or offline and they shape the overall market sentiment in spite of whatever official information may have been spreading out there. But you need to take all the pieces of information and integrate them into one consideration. Yup, you would need to perform something called *"sentiment analysis"*. Remember, it is entirely up to you to scale the sense of the market. After this, you need to decide how you want to integrate your view of the market sentiment and put it into your trading strategy.

Take note, *"sentiment analysis"* could be a fundamental instrument in your toolbox. This is because sentiment is a considerable element that drives the movements in the market of trading. Also, remember that you are never able to dictate what the market should do. All you need to do is create a calculated response which factors in taking control of the market. Thus, by including sentiment analysis in your trading tools, you will be assisted in deciding the appropriate action. Otherwise, there will be a high possibility of making losses if you choose not to pay attention to sentiment analysis. Hence, it is justifiable to say that this sentiment analysis is crucial for you to become a profitable trader.

Note:
1. Be informed about the trade both officially and by word of mouth
2. Understand the key factors affecting the trade

Rollercoaster Trading and Risk Tolerance Approach

Momentum trading is another technique for you to consider. Momentum traders buy and sell trade depending on the current price movement using the historical movement as a reference. The price of the trade has a peak and trough momentum at which the price will move intensely in a specified direction until the tendency eventually loses its strength and runs in the opposite direction. In these modern days, momentum strategies in trading are well-known and commonly used in both the public and academic worlds to gauge when to buy or sell the trade. Plus, it is applicable for both short and long term approaches.

Note:
1. Find out the historical movement of the trade
2. Identify the peak and trough points

Trading System of Law

Rule-based trading is a basic and straightforward strategy. It consists of the facts or ideas within the *'informational overload'* produced by market participants instead of grounding the decisions only on responsive *'gut feelings'*. The rule-based trading system is based on intelligent algorithms that have progressed throughout a long history of what works and what has failed.

A robust system of rule-based trading can steer you away from the attraction to buy an overvalued trade. By right with this rule-based trading strategy, you should know and understand what trade you should buy. There are two essential things to take note of here:

- The foremost important consideration is a thoughtful attitude in any company as well as the market
- Your tolerance for potential risk

Note:
1. Construct a trading plan
2. Set your targets
3. Follow your plan

Oscillating Trading

Swing trading generally takes less time than other forms of trading. It is important to identify and consider the duration of the display. Swing trading might be an excellent option for you if you want to do trades alongside your permanent job. Swing traders buy or sell along with price instability. Swing trades can hold for one day or weeks at a time and they tend to display for a briefer time than tendency trades.

Swing trading's main goal is to capture a large piece of prospective price progress in a single move. Depending on the individual risk level, some traders may target unpredictable stocks with plenty of fluctuation while other traders might have a preference for more dignified stocks. In a different circumstance, swing trading can be defined as the process of recognizing where the price of a trade is most likely going to move, inflowing a site, and then capturing a large piece of the profit as a result of that movement.

Note:
1. Identify which stock to target
2. Study the uptrend and downtrend of the stock
3. Set your buy, sell and stop-loss price

Example of Swing Trade in AAPL:

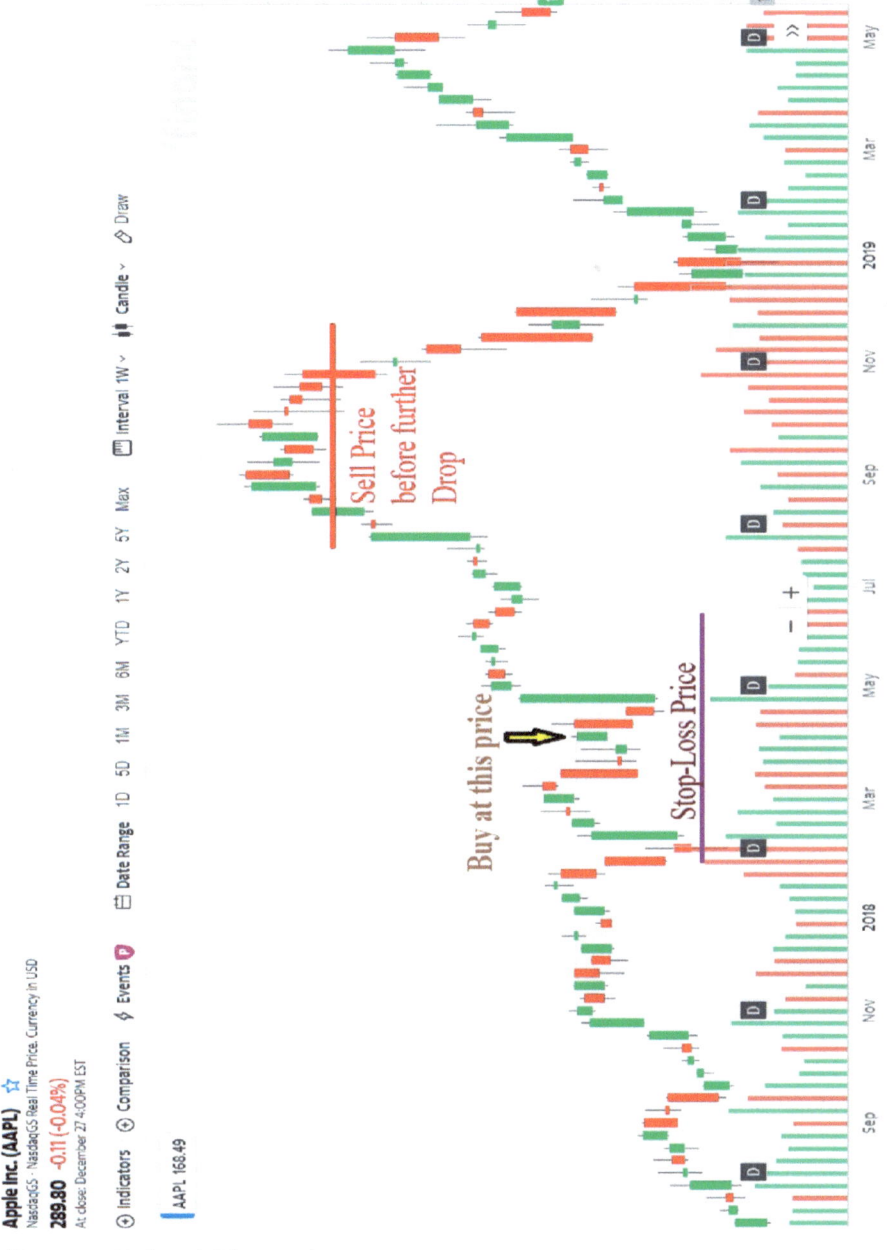

(Source: Yahoo! Finance)

Maximizing Your Money Per Trade

Interested in buying stocks from various industries but don't have the capital? Index trading is the solution! A group of stocks forms index trading. Usually, the investor considers an investment of assets with different conditions that they want to place resources into. In addition to this, the investor considers the valuation of both the profit and loss which determines the moving assessment of the purchased resources.

Interested in more than one stock but don't have enough capital? Should you stop there and wait to accumulate your investment funds?

NO!

You shouldn't do that as you will miss the opportunity to earn more during the wait.

There are a few options for you to choose:
1. Invest in just one stock (Gain ownership)
2. Invest in an index fund (Leverage your money)

When we are discussing trade, there are a lot of different available strategies for every single person who is interested in trading index selections. But what is a 'put' or 'call' on the index? These terms are used when buying the index to describe whether it's going up or down. The purchase is named as a 'call' if the index price is going up. On the other hand, 'put' is the purchase term for buying when the index price is going down.

Note:
1. Identify your risk level
2. Do you want to diversify your portfolio?
3. Identify which stock to buy: one company stock or a basket of stocks

Example of Index Fund: Vanguard 500 Index Investor (VFINX)

(Source: Yahoo! Finance)

Activity #1

True or False

1) I should trade using my 'gut' feelings. [T / F]
2) It is not important to observe historical trade movement. [T / F]
3) Index trading is formed by a basket of stocks. [T / F]
4) I should identify my risk level. [T / F]
5) I need to have a trade portfolio. [T / F]
6) I should buy trade at 'high' price and sell at 'low' price. [T / F]

Answers for Activity #1

True or False

1) I should trade using my 'gut' feelings. **(False)**
   You need to have a proper trading plan and follow the plan unless you are a fortune-teller who has the superpower to foresee the next market price.

2) It is not important to observe historical trade movement. **(False)**
   You need to observe the historical trade movement (at least a period of 5 years) to understand the peak and trough of the trade. Analyze the historical trade movement to set your 'buy' and 'sell' price.

3) An index fund is formed by a basket of stocks. **(True)**
   An index fund consists of a basket of different stocks. It can be a portfolio of different industries or focused on one industry with different companies.

4) I should identify my risk level. **(True)**
   Understand your risk level, so that you could plan how much you are prepared to lose (stop-loss) and how much you want to gain (sell).

5) I need to have a trade portfolio. **(True)**
   Having a trading portfolio is useful to record your risk and trades as well as the diversification.

6) I should buy trade at 'high' price and sell at 'low' price. **(False)**
   You should buy trade at 'low' price and sell at 'high' to gain profits.
   Hint: *In a situation when the price drops 20% or more than your buy price, you can consider continuing to buy if it is a more dignified*

stock where you know the company will not go out of business or bankrupt.

Chapter 2

The #1 Mistake You May Make Which Kills Your Profits

Can you aim to become a successful trader?

Yes!

To do this, you need to have the capability to differentiate between good as well as bad trading strategies. The most precise method to gauge success is to view both the profits along with the losses that may occur for any specified strategy. But there are other essential things to be considered when deciding a trading strategy.

One thing to keep in mind is that trading strategies ought to be personal and fixed along your journey with whatever farfetched situations which may occur. This is due to the markets being extremely unpredictable as well as the volatility of the period. Loads of traders execute various hazardous trading strategies which may not be the best choice for you. If you are trying to copy another person's trading strategy then you ought to find the constituents of that strategy. You also need to consider managing the risk as well; only settle on a strategy if this is suitable for you.

Remember to analyze if you are not content with the type of trade and/or positioning of the trades according to the rules set within the strategy you're using. Ultimately, when you choose another person's strategy, it doesn't really matter whether the strategy has long-term prosperity anticipation or not. It would definitely be difficult for you to go after the rules and you might not attain the most favorable results.

The Strategy of Scheduling Options

This one is also known as "calendar spreads". As soon as there are certain crumble conditions in the market, different options are a precious tool designed for investors. Do you know the facts of "options"? There are a lot of options strategies accessible which could help to reduce the instability risk of the market. The calendar spread is one of these methods. It has been known as a method to be practiced for the duration of any market ambiance. It is an excellent method to unite the advantages delivered by the spreads along with directional options trades in a similar site.

The first step in scheduling a trade: You need to analyze the sentiment of the market with a few months of prediction. Forecast the market! If a trader has a bearish view of the market, the trader should consider setting a calendar spread once he/she has determined the buy price. This strategy is perfect for being applied toward a stock, index, or other Exchange Trading Fund (ETF). To get better results, the trader may find some important information related to the trade and business in the middle of the bid and request prices. The final steps occupied in this process are intended for the trader to set up a plan to open outlets as well as manage their risk appropriately.

Price Action and Profitability

The price action demonstrates the characteristics of the security price movements. The movement is similar when categorized and analyzed on the price changes history. The recent and actual price is subjective of trading decision-based indicators. The fundamental analysis factors and focus are on the recent price movement. The trading strategy and price action are dependent on technical analysis tools.

Price action trading is related to historical data and price movements. It is a proper and systematic trading practice that uses technical analysis tools with the recent price history. The technical analysis tools are trend lines, charts, and swings while advanced trading includes price bars, complex combinations, and breakouts with the volatility indications. Analytic traders interpret the rules and behavior of the trade before making decisions.

To be a successful trader, you need to understand business waves. The trading positions and scenarios are subjective to psychological and behavioral states. Price action trading defines the approach of price speculation and predictions. Business development and growth are based on the arbitrageurs and speculators. The information is used for a wide range of securities that include derivatives, equities, forex, bonds, and commodities. Price action trading also includes a combination of different options. Other options are related to observations such as trading patterns, stop-losses, exit, and entry levels. Below are the scenarios that involve two-step processes:

1. Identify the scenario by considering the stock price, breakout, and channel range.
2. Identify trading opportunities, such as stock, retreating, and overshoot conditions.
3. Price action trading is limited to profit trading instead of long-term investments.
4. The advantages include self-defined strategies that offer flexibility to the traders.
5. The traders are in charge allowing the strategy to decide actions while they just follow the rules.

Trading Edge Over the Market

A trading edge is an observation approach, a special technique in theory to create an advantage. Traders can create cash advantages and can trade to achieve positive results. The cynical objective is to create a trading edge. It can be used to estimate the profit and success of the business in local and international markets. Traders can learn and apply the techniques to gain profits in a higher probability. A reasonable critique identifies the issues in the business and the way to find some "holy grail" to make a profit. The statement of "using a trading edge over the market" is questionable for different reasons that are mentioned below:

1. The assumptions that are underpinning this type of flawed thinking.
2. Some traders use positive trading outcomes on a consistent and sustainable basis.

So, how do you create your trading edge?

You may start by identifying the moving trend in the market because you should trade based on the direction of current trade trends. When should you buy? You can start to buy trades in the downtrend or you can set a range boundary of the trade, buy at the lower range and sell at the upper range. Even with a trading edge set, there is still a chance of having a losing trade, but having a trading edge could increase the probability of gaining profits. Practice your trading technique using a demo account or in the real market and you will find which direction of the trend will result in profit with a higher probability.

Although it is correct that several techniques can be used to work over different criteria, traders may fail due to behavioral issues. It is often said that in the field of business, those who get success are the people who do not like to fail. All traders do have common characteristics but these differ from successful traders. There are many reasons for the success of a trader, such as education, experience, and being serious in this trade. Some investors invest by using a trading software system, or they may choose to start with the proven trading strategies, trade with the discount broker of choice, or even join the events which connect traders.

Low-Risk Options Trading Strategy

The successful traders will always test out models with different strategies. The best model is low risk with a high probability of profitable trades. Models can simulate the results by applying different trading strategies on historical data. It is important to analyze what would happen if an investor applied investment strategy X during the period of Y.

Each trader has a different risk tolerance level. In general terms, low risk doesn't mean that the investor is not willing to take any risk-related action, but it also defines the trading capital available. The statistical trading process is used to generate the average loss and average win-rate. Based on risk tolerance, statistical consideration generates an average rate of win and loss. The edge comes for the application of the management of money. Low-risk trades provide low returns while on the other hand, higher risk trades offer more returns at the end. Selecting risk and reward is easy with the option delta formula.

$$Delta\ Formula = \frac{Change\ in\ Price\ of\ the\ Asset}{Change\ in\ Price\ of\ the\ Underlying}$$

Trading with low-risk and high-profit probability, you need to choose the options which are more useful. Based on the view of the market, buyer options, trade structure, and other strategies, there are several options for investment with the consideration of high volatility and seller options. In stock trading, the time consideration is not as important as the option of buying. Theoretically, you can hold the stock forever, but for the trade options buyers, the time decay becomes an enemy.

High-Profit Probability Options Trading Strategy

When judging a strategy, it is not enough to just look at the profit factor that is only divided into the outcomes of the business. So, it is important to look for and to find low-risk and high probability trades. There are many stock and index categories that are divided into eight factors and states. The states of 2, 4, 6, and 8 are the bearish states and on the contrary, states 1 and 8 are the extremes. Before investing, one must consider buying "in the money" and "out of the money" options. The general rule of the thumb is used when considering the buying options: The higher consideration is to find the option of trade and probability that ends with profits.

In the case of business, a 100% profit target is selected with different positions of trade. The system must look for the nearest delta values of the trade, different categories which include flexibility and the leverage of options. The options consider a great investment with the selection of flexibility. You can hedge a long position and use the leverages for proper and pure speculation. In both and either case, you can reduce the risk of purchasing options. The risk of trading options can be controlled and minimized. The key factor of low-risk and high-probability trading is to know and understand the quantification of risk. In business, one must have the ability to analyze historical data and use this analysis to inform decisions. The risk is linked with the relative statement. The risk tolerance can be used to develop models that suit the investment objective. When considering the combined effect and state modeling, you can find low risk and high probability trades.

Be a Fortune Teller by Using Price and Volume

Some normal volume attributes can confirm the price of doing business in the market. The important factors are mentioned below:

1. Before congestion, it is important to analyze that the volume is highest including the pennant, channels, triangle, and flag.
2. If the volume is lowest then it goes deeper into congestion.
3. A valid breakout is used to increase the volume of business with congestion. The subsidies are considered higher from many folds and the trend becomes higher.
4. The volume of business increases with major reversals.
5. The volume and trend become higher and dry up in the counter-trend. Then, the volume should move with the trend.
6. In the formations of double or triple top and bottom, the volume reaches reversal conditions and congestion must slow down.

7. There is a specific relation between the attributes of volume and price and the direction of price changes with the volume.

In the case of heavier volume, the price level is lower which can change the congestion formation. On the other hand, if the heavier volume occurs, it results in a higher price level. The formation of congestion can change the price and eventually decline the lower support level for the congestion pattern. The heavy volume will lower the edges and take control of the protracted distribution period. The volume and the direction of price can be used as a predictive condition. It is expected that the breakout volume must increase with the increasing trend of price in the business. If the volume is greater, on the other hand, it will change the trend and reverse the process in the opposite direction.

The usual situation comprises of high volume and can be used to treat countertrends at a low rate. The violent price and wide bar swings along the higher volume conditions and the price are supposed to be kept at reverse. Before investing in the business, there is a large bar with multiple violent prices and the swing of the volume is higher. Always consider the countertrend volume that is higher as compared to the trending volume. The volume spikes show a downward and upward price pressure. The upward price movement changes with the volume price. There are small ranges of bars that show resistance and decline in a large volume. The price trend with the subsequent price is given below in the table and one must consult the table before deciding on the business.

Price Trend	Price Trend	Subsequent Price
Falling	Reversing up	Up
Falling	Accelerating downward	Up
Congested or flat	Breakout to downside	Down
Congested or flat	Breakout to upside	Up
Rising	Breaking down	Down
Rising	Up and accelerating	Down

Activity #2

True or False

1) Higher risk leads to lower returns. [T / F]
2) Low risk with high returns is not possible. [T / F]
3) Flat price trend → Downside price trend [T / F]
   → Subsequent price is up.
4) Having a trading edge increases the probability to gain profits. [T / F]
5) I can copy any successful trader's trade strategy. [T / F]

Answer for Activity #2

True or False

1) Higher risk leads to lower returns. **(False)**
   Actually, a higher risk leads to higher returns, but at the same time, it also leads to higher losses. For example, 50% risk level = 50% gains = 50% losses.

2) Low risk with high returns is not possible. **(False)**
   Low risk with high returns is possible if you choose the right options with more versatility.

3) Flat price trend → Downside price trend → Subsequent price is up. **(False)**
   The answer is that the subsequent price would be down as per the table guideline provided, but if you have encountered an unusual situation, the result might differ.

4) Having a trading edge increases the probability to gain profits. **(True)**
   Set a range boundary of the trade, buy at the lower range and sell at the upper range to increase the probability of gaining profits.

5) I can copy any successful trader's trade strategy. **(False)**
   You need to analyze the strategy and risk level. Only apply the strategy if it is suitable for you.

Chapter 3

Ultimate Bargain Hunter

Trading Crude Oil and Natural Gas

Should you find some strategies used by successful business people?

YES!

Those successful business people who gain profits by applying simple investment strategies are worth following. Making decisions based on business is dependent on conditions using the moving average. For example, using the average daily bank deposits, the company's daily sales performance is revealed. An investor should view the stock prices daily as an insight into the business instead of just numbers and symbols. An investment decision can be decided based on the Federal Reserve Bank index in the United States or using the financial statement of price and value. Business trade in the news is always associated with the risk. If the business head does not have good decisions and better strategies then it can cause losses in the business.

In the present day, investors use inventory reports of crude oil and natural gas to change their strategies. Crude oil inventory reports which record the change in the barrels of crude oil are released by the Energy Information Administration (EIA). The actual inventory reports are linked with the forecast projections under the given analysis. The binary option is another market relative that defines the period and strike price. An important strategy for trading crude oil is to use the binary options trade that has an indicative price. A new investor can apply successful business steps used by previous investors in the market. Consider the following example for successful trade in the oil industry:

1. In the time frame of 9:00 to 11:00, the crude oil company was selected for trade.

2. At 10:16 am, two more OTM traders were involved in the underlying price of the market.
   a. Purchased crude oil at > 48.42 with maximum reward $80.50 and maximum risk $19.50.
   b. Sell crude oil at >46.82 with maximum reward $ 79.25 and maximum risk $ 20.75.

In this process, the maximum risk was subtracted from the maximum reward and a successful trade was carried out by becoming a good buyer and seller in the stock market.

A similar process can be considered for the natural gas business. The Energy Information Administration (EIA) releases a report about natural gas storage. Now consider the spike up and down for the trade sideways. Consider if the market moves significantly in one direction and the other direction is a valuable contract and trade. The contract expires with the maximum and minimum conditions of profit. Sometimes, the trade acts as a hedge that is against the other trade.

Trading With Time-Bard

It is often questioned that if intellect and hard work are enough to get you only so far, then what are the factors that can continue to make you a successful investor? There are some other factors and approaches that have tremendous correlation and follow the process or steps of investors in the market which can help you.

A successful trader dedicates their time and effort to analyzing historical data. What can be achieved by doing that? You can gain insight into how a market's past behavior can relate to its future. The market behavior can only be studied by historical data analysis. The volatility, price, and volume elements are used to measure and study the market over a defined period. The analysis of historical data commonly uses four key aspects of the price:

Open: The first price traded at the beginning of a given period.

Close: The last price traded at the end of a given period.

High: The highest price traded during a given period.

Low: The lowest price traded during a given period.

The price values of open, close, high and low are crucial in trading analysis for defining trading strategies. With modern technology, there are various investment applications that provide statistical data. You can choose data for a certain number of days, weeks, months, and even years. So, how much data horizon is enough for your analysis?

Well, that depends on your trading strategy. Are you trading for short-term, mid-term, or long-term? But no matter which term you are choosing, volatility is very important. Why? Because you can only gain profits by buying low and selling high. A stock with no volatility, what can you gain from it? Nothing, unless there are dividends.

Below are some horizon recommendations:

Short-term: 1 to 3 years

Mid-term: 3 to 5 years

Long-term: 5 years or more

But what method is the best? The answer is to study the whole history of the market if you have the time and capability to do it. Because "history tends to repeat itself", it is best if you are well prepared or it.

Stock and Forex Trading

It is often observed that many traders make mistakes as they are short-term thinkers and only think about the next trade instead of the present trade and investment. They never consider the overall edge and trading a Forex business produces over the market. Below are the important five steps to overcome issues using the edge of price action in order to generate success.

1. Focus on the story of price action and statement for the trends, supports, trader, and flow of the business.
2. Trigger one price action at the perfect time.
3. For a successful business, become like a sniper behind the bushes instead of a machine gunner that is wideout in an open area.
4. Work down in different time frames and not identify the other way.
5. Before investing in the market, develop a pre-trade plan.

Activity #3

True or False

1) Create a trading plan after you invest in the market.   [T / F]
2) The "close" price is the same as the lowest price traded.   [T / F]
3) The Energy Information Administration (EIA) provides oil & gas reports.   [T / F]
4) Use 1 to 3 years of historical data for a mid-term investment. [T / F]
5) I can trade focusing on the trends and flow of the business only.   [T / F]

Answers for Activity #3

True or False

1) Create a trading plan after you invest in the market. (**False**)
   You should develop a pre-trade plan before investing in the market.

2) The "close" price is the same as the lowest price traded. (**False**)
   The "close" price is the last price traded.

3) The Energy Information Administration (EIA) provides (**True**)
   oil & gas reports.
   The Energy Information Administration (EIA) releases crude oil and natural gas inventory reports.

4) Use 1 to 3 years of historical data for a mid-term investment. (**False**)
   It is recommended to use 3 to 5 years of historical data for a mid-term investment.

5) I can trade focusing on the trends and flow of the business (**False**)
   only.
   You need to trade focusing on the price action and statement for the trends, supports, trader, and flow of the business.

Chapter 4

Money That Loses Trades

It is a common fact that despite all the available information and knowledge, still most traders are not able to succeed in the trading business and they lose their money.

For example, in Forex trading, the majority of traders make several mistakes. They invest money in a way in which they only get losing trades in the end, leading to their ultimate failure. So, they leave the field of trading because they think that they cannot take any successful steps. Traders must understand WHY they lose money and HOW they used their money to lose trade. Traders must understand that money should be invested by keeping certain things in mind, otherwise, they will end up on the losing side. This is what happens with the majority of traders.

So, the question is: WHAT should they do? And the simple answer is that they should keep certain ideas in mind to avoid losing trade. They should identify the reasons which played a part in their failure or loss of trade. Once a trader will be able to look at those things then the process would become easier for him/her to make good returns. It is not something impossible to achieve, rather it can be achieved with a little wisdom, knowledge, and the correct thought process.

The #1 Mistake Approach

The first thing that traders should keep in mind is that they should never try to beat the market. Remember, the market is something way broader than your expectations. To be a success in the market, you need to understand the different dynamics of the market and define different trends that lead to a better path. If you are going with a mindset that you will beat the market then your failure is an obvious result waiting to happen. No one has ever beaten the market because the market itself is something that is way beyond the reach of a trader. You can take so many benefits from the market, but you can't beat it.

The second most important reason which plays its part in losing trades is that the start-up capital is low by the trader. The mistake made by traders is that they invest a smaller amount of capital with expectations of high returns. From a short term perspective, they may achieve it, but they may only get it once or twice. From a long term perspective, they cannot continue to do it. This strategy is leading them to a complete disaster because they will end up losing all the money.

The #1 Negligence You May Have Made

Risk management is crucial in trading and this is where most traders get it all wrong. They tend to make decisions that cannot manage risks accordingly, so they ultimately lose their trade in the market. If you want to survive in the trading market then risk management is the most essential thing to have. There can be a situation where you are a great trader with good enough information to gain profits in the market, but if you're making decisions regarding risk management and you don't have any skills, this is where the decision can be made in the wrong direction. In trading, earning profit is not the ultimate goal, rather the real objective should also be to protect what you have earned. You should know when risks are looming around and what you have to do in such situations to remain safe from any disaster. Other traders lose their trade because they become greedy. They want to get every possible penny from the market and squeeze it as much as possible. Such a greedy plan never works in the end and traders fail.

You may lose your trade and money because you are always confused about the future course of action. An indecisive trading mind can never prosper in the trading market. If you are unable to make wise decisions, you will lose the whole plot. For example, in a situation where a trader has invested some amount in trade, they tend to retract the trade once they see that things not going well in the beginning. This is not the right approach. Once you have entered the market, you need to give some time for things to happen. Success never comes overnight and it always takes time.

The other considerable reason which plays its part in losing trade is the fact that the traders are not ready to accept their mistakes. We have seen various instances where a trader has made a mistake and taken the wrong direction, but he/she is not ready to admit his/her mistake. If you cannot accept your mistakes then you stop learning at that particular moment. Mistakes are not bad to make if you take them seriously and learn from them so they are not repeated in the future.

How to plan risk management? Here's one of the most simplified methods to plan your risk. Ask yourself: How much are you willing to lose per trade? That will set your risk tolerance. For example, you have invested $1,000 in the trade. You can afford to lose $500 of the trade. Your risk tolerance would be 50% ($500 ÷ $1,000) and you can then set a stop-loss price.

But if you are trading in a particularly reputable company and you have analyzed that the company is financially stable, you might want to take a risk to further invest in the company even though the trade price has dropped.

Slow Down Your Pace

There have been more surprising facts to reveal why most traders lose the game in the trading market. A lot of reasons for losing trades have been mentioned earlier and a few more can also be emphasized for traders to know what they have to avoid in the trading market. The first major thing is that the majority of traders enter into the trading market with an expectation of making quick profits. They come here with some dreams in mind and think that trading will help them get rich in no time. It is absolutely a false perception amongst the majority of traders because there is no short cut to achieve big dreams.

It has been observed in different surveys that around 40% of traders stay in the market for around one month and they quit in the essence of disappointment. The people who last for more than one month and try to stay firm in the market have an 80% chance of losing their patience in 2 years. It is quite shocking to know that only 7% of traders remain in the market for more than 5 years. It shows how traders come up with the wrong perceptions and expectations thus getting disappointed so early. This leaves the field open for those who are here to stay for the long term. Trading is not a game of emotions or idealism. Rather it is a proper field that needs a high IQ level, research and analysis, as well as the ability to understand different methods of trading. You cannot come and conquer the trading market. You have to be wise, careful, decisive, a risk-taker, and patient, otherwise, your money is going to lose trades.

Swing Trading

There are various strategies to deal with losses or to gain returns in the trading field. It is up to a trader's choice to choose which strategy is suitable for him/her. The situations can be different as well as the mindset of the traders as it is important to understand that in every given situation, a trader must analyze different factors to make a viable decision regarding his/her strategy. One such strategy is called "swing trading". Traders need to understand what swing trading is. It is a strategy that basically has its focus on getting smaller returns or gains in a short period so that profits can be earned and losses recovered. It is good to know that returns are made with the help of this strategy, but they will always be smaller in percentage.

Moreover, a trader needs to be able to identify different market factors to adopt a swing trading strategy. These smaller profits can turn into handsome annual returns in the end. Mostly, such a trading position is taken for around two weeks, but it can stay longer as well depending upon the situation of the market. So, it means that when a trader targets the market with swing trading, he/she does not go for 20 to 30%, rather the objective is to get returns of up to

5 to 10%. So, if you are looking to make handsome smaller returns in the market then swing trading is the way to go.

The Technique to Avoid Pitfalls

If any strategy is adopted in the trading business then it is vital to keep in mind that every strategy can have its pitfalls. That is the case with swing trading as well. It is not that traders will always have a win-win situation with swing trading, but they can also face great risk if they make any wrong decisions. It has been observed that swing traders make a few common mistakes when they go with the swing trading method. So, they must identify those mistakes so that mistakes can be avoided. The first mistake made by swing traders is that they always keep watching the market too closely. They will always analyze the stocks and prices all day long whereas even stocks should be given some space to breathe. The other mistake made by swing traders is that they keep making small decisions without any proper thought process. They do not think much and make immediate decisions that may pay off, but when such decisions go wrong, they can be disastrous.

Traders must understand that trading is a serious business that requires a lot of skills throughout the process as well as patience. You have to be disciplined in both approaches and patience. Swing traders lack such attributes and when they make decisions it proves them wrong the majority of the time. One more pitfall of swing trading is that the traders just focus on profits and returns. They think that small moves would be good enough to earn profits whereas there are always some risks to look for. They don't manage risk and end up trapped in the worst situation. If traders want to become successful then it is viable to adopt a risk managing strategy. Swing traders can avoid all of these pitfalls by making a proper trading plan. This should involve a lot of thought processes as well as research so that the right decisions are made in the end.

Activity #4

True or False

1) I can beat the market. [T / F]
2) I should continue using the same methodology [T / F]
   even though, I just lost in the trade.
3) I need to include risk management in my strategy. [T / F]
4) Patience is golden. [T / F]
5) I should give up once the trade is not going well. [T / F]

Answers for Activity #4

True or False

1) I can beat the market. **(False)**
   No one has ever beaten the market because the market itself is depending on the demand and supply. Just one man can't win a troupe.

2) I should continue using the same methodology **(False)**
   even though I just lost in the trade.
   You need to reflect and analyze what went wrong. Improve your strategy.

3) I need to include risk management in my strategy. **(True)**
   Risk management is required for you to set your stop-loss price and know your risk appetite.

4) Patience is golden. **(True)**
   Trading is not a game of emotions or idealism. You need to analyze the trade trend and know when to exit and enter the market.

5) I should give up once the trade is not going well. **(False)**
   You should reflect and analyze what went wrong, not give up. Embrace your mistakes and improve your strategy. That is the right action.

Chapter 5

Strategy of Payment

Reading Order Flow

A successful business depends on the option and contract between the seller and buyer. There are two possible options, including 'puts' and 'calls':

1. Calls give a right to the buyer and he is not under any kind of obligation. The process depends on the buyer power and specific stock or financial instrument. The business contract is associated with the specified price, strike price, specific date, and expiration date of the contract. The buyer has the right to buy any business associated with the strike price and the seller obligation is based on the conditions that are required to be met.
2. Puts also give rights to the buyer but without any obligation. Puts are considered to sell the services under the strike price on and before expiration. Put buyers have no obligation and no right. They are not selling to underly stock and the strike price is prior to different conditions of expiration. On the other hand, if the put seller is under obligation to buy underlying conditions, the strike price must exercise the rights of buyers and sellers.

So, the question here is how to determine the options and price? There are six factors and price inputs that determine some premium options. The options include the stock price, dividends, the strike price of the options, interest rates, the time remaining until expiration, and implied volatility.

In general, the stock fluctuation in the prices is observed weekly and daily. At this point, the options will be more expensive and tend to be more expensive due to certain conditions. The earning reports and major announcements decrease with the price sharply after the announcement. The best example is biotech stocks and drug announcements. One option is traded conditions for one or two reasons. The speculation hedges against a stock position. The option is bought as a speculation for the stock and how it will move in the specified direction. Calls can be purchased because of the belief of a trader in the stock that it will move higher before getting the expiration dates. Option strike prices have a relation with the different terms including "in the money", "at the money" and "out of the money".

1. The call "in the money" occurs when the stock price is higher than the strike price.
2. The call "out of the money" occurs when the stock price is lower as compared to the strike price.
3. The call "at the money" occurs it means that the strike price is the same and equal to the stock price.

The invest of puts is the condition of strike price in the business and it can be considered as to be "in the money". The alternative option is put as "out of the money" that occurs if the strike price is low as compared to the stock price. The "at the money" condition is similar to the calls.

Here, let's discuss the options that are purchased to the hedge against the stock positions. The trade is higher in real-time conditions and it could be a speculative play. The experience of a successful business is based on the stock position. The trading condition is considered to learn and read about the conditions and decisions in the market.

In the business, certainly, there is a specific combination of science and art that is related to the skills and trading strategy. Considering the big stock options and orders, it could be dubbed as an "Unusual Options Activity".

Unusual Option Activity

There is no specified secret of becoming a profitable trader. One must consider the skeptical conditions before telling others. The technique is being considered and outlined with the text conditions. The profitable techniques watched by successful tycoons are unusual options activity and the reading order flow which generates a trading floor. An example of a successful trader is someone who demonstrated his skills after having experience in Apple stock and AAPL. These stocks' turnover and profit were in millions of dollars. Merrill Lynch is the broker in the stock exchange and he considers pit and sells strategy for AAPL spreads. His strategy is known as "HES" based on the long and selling volatility for the profitable trades. There is a combination of overflow with technical indicators such as Ichimoku Cloud. He devised his OCRRBTT trading plan that enabled him to have a successful and profitable trade in the stock market.

The OCRRBTT Trading Plan

The plan is often pronounced as "Oak RIBBIT" and it is a strategy of trading in the stock market. The plan is based on the step-by-step method for trading with the usual and low condition option activities. After having an evaluation of the unusual trading plans, one will be able to consider all the options and decide which option could be followed and what can be ignored in the trade. The acronym letters stand for open interest, chart, risk, reward, breakeven, time, and target.

1. Open interest
For a successful business, one must consider the open interest and trade volume with the current open interest. The opening position and the worth of taking condition depend on the activity. Only consider trades that have greater volume as compared to the open interest.

2. Chart
The second option is to consider the opening order and look at the chart with the underlying stock. The question here is if the stock is in the bearish or strong bullish trend? What if support and resistance strike at the institution of

trading? What are the speculating ups and downsides of the business that could lead to any hedge in the business? Before investing in any business, you must consider all the factors if you want to have successful trades in the market.

3. Risk, Reward, Breakeven

After determining the direction of trade, one must evaluate the risk and reward profile of the institution along with their risk tolerance level. Sometimes the trade could be very risky for the average retail trader. If you find significant support or any significant resistance in the breakeven point then reconsider the strategy.

4. Time and Target

Before investing, one must be careful of potential catalyst events that can induce an impact on the business. It is important to have the proper and overall direction of the stock and to know of any near term catalyst events such as product launches, drug announcements, and earnings. These factors might create an impact on the decision of trading. After setting the time horizon, you have to identify the profit target. Here, think about if you are leaving the trade on the expiration? Taking off rest ride or half at a double business? Knowing the answers will help decide and manage the process forward.

In the end, the trade must end up as a fantastic winner. The motivation behind the trade is to become more experienced in the trade.

Perks of Scheduled Options

The strategy of scheduled options considers factors with a four-time condition each year when ears perk up with the equity and stock options. Similar to clockwork, the gears of business start-up and turn tend to be increased or decreased. The earning season schedule is defined in any big-name companies such as Tesla, Apple, Google, and Netflix. In the earning season, the stock market identifies the spikes in volatility and profit potentials. The traders consider all the horizons of weather. The traders in stock use charts and equity options to look for an advantage in the business. The clock condition and stock movements are related to each other. What happens if one changes, does the other do the same? This question is related to each quarter of the business and sets aside the handful of hours that are related to the execution option. The overnight profit potential must be considered in the range of 25 to 30 percent.

If the profit changes during the trading conditions, the beauty is to prepare for the earning seasons.

Maximize Your Profits in the Earning Season

The earning season is the time that is around the beginning of each financial quarter with the companies that are publicly traded. It depends on the previous earning reports of the previous quarter.

The Catch
Despite what you hear from traders related to the equity trader options, the best strategy is to consider the actual earning number instead of the issue. The company makes a profit and does not calculate the money. It is important to consider the reaction of investors on the news.

Identify the important parts of the plan such as the knee jerk reaction of the investors in the stock market.

The negative and positive numbers in the stock represent the situation of dumping and jumping in the business. The moves can be an opportunity at different levels. The best alternative strategy is to consider the reaction on stock price along with the earning numbers.

Four-Step Earning Season Profit Plan

The options in the straddle blows the minds of traders. The first consideration is to pick the stock moves instead of stock directions.

Volatility

The volatility is the amount of market action that considers the market waves and the price fluctuation in the stock experience.

The bigger the reaction, the better it is

It doesn't matter if the stock price reaction is positive or negative, one must consider the way to move dramatically.

Trading in both directions?

Before investing, consider both directions of the option at the same time. If you straddle the market price, what will be the stock movement and profits matter?

Stalk your prey

The first and foremost condition is to stalk the prey and monitor the market movements. Find some ideas from the previous earning reports and quarter conditions of business.

Trading Edge in Simple Steps

For every trader in the market, having the edge over the market is the foremost condition for long-term success. Besides all the other factors, the most powerful factor in business is the good or bad luck of investors. If the trader is lucky enough, even without having an edge in the side market, he can make the trade successfully without losing any investment. The best example of an edge is the game played within casinos. The prime cause is the regular and consistent profits that are generated by playing games and gambling. The games provide chances to win, for instance, by using poker machines and playing blackjack.

You must consider trading in the Forex business! It has more edge over the market and takes high as well as successful price actions.

Keep focusing the price action story

As a price action trader, you have to think about the price actions. It would be better to have a super obvious statement to make, but before investing, consider doing a quick Google search to find major forums that have discussions of price action trading and include the thinking of traders. This will provide a trading pattern that is simple but works like the last one and two candles in the charts. The trade must be based on the last candle that is super important in the market. Consider important and successful price action trade based on ideas extracted from the flow, support, trends, trade behavior, and resistance in the live price action.

Trigger one perfect price action
To obtain a successful and high probability trade, take A+ price action trade. In this way, you will first find a strong trend, what is the price rejecting resistance and support? Is there any kind of space for the price movement and is it a good idea to trade?

When you consider all the factors, just pull the trigger to initiate all the setups. It is more important to make one trigger that gets success in the market instead of a sequence of investments and losing trade.

Now you must be happy that you have tamed and mastered the ability to make successful business trades. After getting success, repeat the same process and trigger the next signal in the market.

Activity #5

True or False

1) Four factors determine premium options. [T / F]
2) "Out of the money" is when the stock price is higher than the strike price. [T / F]
3) The earning season is after each company's quarterly financial reports. [T / F]
4) You must find a positive stock price reaction. [T / F]
5) Get intel by Google searching forums with price action trading topics. [T / F]

Answers for Activity #5

True / False

1) Four factors determine premium options. **(False)**
   Six factors determine premium options. These are the stock price, dividends, the strike price of the options, interest rates, the time remaining until expiration, and implied volatility.

2) "Out of the money" is when the stock price is higher than the strike price. **(False)**
   The call "out of the money" occurs when the stock price is lower compared to the strike price.

3) The earning season is after each company's quarterly financial reports. **(False)**
   The earning season is around the beginning of each quarterly financial report. It also depends on the previous quarter earning reports.

4) You must find a positive stock price reaction. **(False)**
   The bigger the reaction, the better. It doesn't matter if the stock price reaction is positive or negative, one must consider the way to move dramatically.

5) Get intel by Google searching forums with price action trading topics. **(True)**
   Before investing, consider using Google search to find major forums that include discussions of price action trading and the thinking of traders to find more information.

Conclusion

So, we have reached the end of this informative discussion regarding simplified trading techniques which can be considered for both good and bad times. It was evident after analyzing so many things about trading that profit and loss are the patterns of trading that run on parallel levels. If you have made any profits, then keep in mind that you may face loss as well. To avoid such a bad situation, you have to be careful.

On the other hand, if you are earning losses on your stocks then remember that loss is also not permanent in trading. You can recover the loss by adopting certain considerable techniques and turn any opportunity into a great success. Trading is the game of patience and you have to be wise in every stage. It can be said that trading does not allow one to relax at any stage in any given circumstance. For instance, if you are making good profits and everything is looking fine, you still can't let your guard down because the situation can always change in a couple of hours or weeks. So, always remain proactive in your approach and never let the market to ruin your investment. You need to adopt different trading strategies as well as keep an eye on managerial implications. There are strategies, both for good and bad situations, which have been explained in this guide. You can analyze each strategy to find a roadmap for your future in the trading market.

-- Irvin Ellison

Review Time

If you found what you learned from this guide useful, I'd appreciate your help in passing your lessons forward by going into the link shown below and encouraging others to get this for themselves.

You are more than welcome to give feedback, both positive and negative.

(Amazon may ask you to log in before they allow you to do so):

https://www.amazon.com/dp/B083F4CP9C

www.ingramcontent.com/pod-product-compliance
Lightning Source LLC
Chambersburg PA
CBHW040243220526
45473CB00001B/354